Single, Married and Sexual Lust

Amazon

ISBN (Paperback): **979-836-681-861-2**

Genre: Personal Development

All correspondence should be addressed to...

oppyadex@gmail.com, +2349050730702

Published and printed in Nigeria by

+2348083942528, +2348140131255

#13, Gbajabiamila Street, off Camp Davies Road, Ayobo, Lagos, Nigeria

www.valueplus.ng/publishing

To the Teacher of all teachers, the Holy Spirit who teaches me the principles of the kingdom and grants me grace to collate this treatise for the benefit of God's people. He is always the source of all my inspirations.

To everyone who has a genuine desire for healthy relationships with the opposite gender and a hunger for sexual purity in conformity with the biblical standards.

Endorsements

WHAT OTHERS ARE SAYING ABOUT THIS BOOK

Are you in the grip of the destructive influence of lust? Are you a lesbian or gay and you have been looking for an escape route from such lifestyle? Or you have been eaten up with secret masturbation. I strongly recommend this book for your deliverance. It contains simple but proven principles to run against the wind of lust. It's up to you: If you need help, study this book.

— **Pastor Elmarie**
South Africa.

I really like the way Timothy writes. He is a visionary, and yet has a practical writing style of simplifying complex issues. I highly recommend this book to anyone who desires victory over sexual lust. I picked it up to read few chapters, and it so captivated me that I read the whole book!

— **Feyi Adesanmi**
Teens and Youth Coach, Lagos.

I recommend a book that has changed my life. Before I came across pastor Timothy's book, I have tried all means to be freed from the trap of lust. I kept rising and fallen until I laid my hand on this precious material and learnt the biblical principles. The contents of this book can liberate anyone from the cage of lust if read with an open heart.

— **Engr. Segun Abayomi**
Abuja, Nigeria.

Acknowledgements

THIS BOOK IS A VISION BIRTHED AND EMPOWERED BY HOLY Spirit, committed to print through the contributions of many destiny - supporters to whom I stand indebted; only eternity can repay them.

My endless appreciation goes to the Almighty God who saved and has chosen me as kingdom ambassador to express the glory and beauty of His image. To Him be all the glory, power, honour, dominion and adoration forever and ever, Amen!

To my dearest, lovely and pretty wife, friend and partner in ministry, Temitope Oluwapelumi and our great kids Oba, Prince and Queen, I remain indebted for your immense support. You are the best!

I am highly grateful to my biological parents, Pastor and Mrs. M.O Adebayo who raised me in the way of the Lord and never seized to guide me all along. I am eternally grateful.

My profound gratitude goes to various Heroes of faith whose impact and input gave me inspiration to write this book: first among them is my father in the Lord, the General Overseer of the Gospel Faith Mission International, Pastor (Dr.) E.O. Abina. He is a practical example of humility that the bible teaches. Daddy, I am one of the countless beneficiaries of your words and deeds.

Others are: Pastor Dr. E.T. Oluwayemi, Pastor Peter Awodimila, Evang. (Dr.) E.O. Falade, Pastor Francis Omoniyi, Evang. F.T. Fajobi, Rev'd Dr. Akintayo Suulola, Pastor Gbenga Ayejuyole, Evangelist Ademola Agbeni, Pastor Beloved Alabi, Pastor S.O. Adebayo, Evang. Bayo David, Pastor Rufus Adeyemi, Pastor Stephen Oginni, Pastor Isaiah Oladapo, Pastor Emmanuel Awogbemi, Pastor Adeyeye, Pastor Seyi Adejare, Elder and Mrs. Ologun, Mr. Kayode Ogunsola, Evangelist Mrs. Olumide, Pastor Daramola Emmanuel and Evang. Dr. Orimogunje (of blessed memory). I am highly privileged to be mentored by many great hands.

I sincerely appreciate a well-respected man of God, Pastor Akinola Akinyemi for writing the foreword for this book out of his busy schedules and his fatherly guidance during and after my NYSC service year at Taraba State, Nigeria. He is an Author, Leadership and Planning Coach, Inspirational Speaker and the Senior Pastor of God's Heritage Christian Centre with its Headquarters in Lagos, Nigeria. I cannot but mention my brothers and friends, Pastor Ozokolo Uchenna, Pastor Elvis from Cameroon, Pastor Yomi Adedeji and Evangelist Joel Daramola for their useful contributions and criticisms towards improving the quality of this material.

I thank Pastor Nelson, Elder Luke Ozoko and Brother Henry Ojo, who painstakingly did the proof reading and also edited this work, with all my other friends; who believed in me and have prayed, guided and helped me to discover my potentials and also provided me a platform to deploy it.

Finally, I thank all able members of Rescue Team Mission Network International whose convergence is to train and equip the present generation in all nooks and crannies of the world despite the differences in backgrounds and ministries.

Much love for you guys!

Contents

Foreword

According to this timely book and other relevant researchers, *"...most young men and women, both single and married are caught in the web of lust."*

According to the dictionary, Lust is usually intense or unbridled sexual desire, I want you to take note of the word "desire".

Lust is not from the outside but from the inside of a man or woman. It's from within.

> *"For I know the thoughts that I think toward you, saith the Lord , thoughts of peace, and not of evil, to give you an expected end."*
>
> — **Jeremiah 29:11** KJV

> *"But every man is tempted, when he is drawn away of his own lust, and enticed."*
>
> — **James 1:14** KJV

> *"But each one is tempted when he is carried away and enticed by his own lust."*
>
> — **James 1:14** NASB

> *"Temptation comes from our own desires, which entice us and drag us away."*
>
> **James 1:14, NLT:**

James 1:14 explains that we are given to lust/temptation when we become carried away by our own natural desires.

The first step toward overcoming lust and temptation is to recognize the human tendency to be seduced by our own fleshly desires. No one is exempted from this lust/temptation, it happens daily, but we can be armed with truth to avoid the evil consequences of it.

This book is all about how just anyone can be free from the destructive influence of lust. Holding this book is a great opportunity because, I know it will profit you, the book contains practical, easy to do steps that will help you overcome temptation and evil consequences of lust.

I would like to say that knowledge acquired in this timely book will not only inform you but also go a long way in helping you honor God and receive the honor of God as well in your moral life, relationships and every areas of your life.

One very important aspect of this book is about the author. His life has proven over the years that putting measures in place will help you please God in your moral life as well as your daily walk with God.

Many thanks to Pastor Timothy Adebayo, the author of this wonderful book: SINGLE, MARRIED AND LUST! *(Eight Simple Principles to Overcome Sexual Lust)*.

Thank You for being a blessing to the body of Christ.

I pray that your influence will know no limits in Jesus Name.

Akinola Akinyemi

Akinola Akinyemi

Senior pastor, God's Heritage Christian Centre Lagos, Nigeria.

Introduction

IN THIS AGE AND TIME, THERE IS SO MUCH PRESSURE ON THE young and the young at heart to compromise and to join the multitude to do evil. We live in an era where illicit sex has become so cheap and so common. Sexual purity no longer trends like before. The dignity of virginity is dissipating at an alarming rate in our society. The continuous increase in sexual immorality on a global scale is becoming unbecoming. What a worrisome malady.

But if God destroyed Sodom and Gomorrah because of immoral activities, there is no chance that He will spare this generation at all.

Jesus was so stirred up that He gave a chilling recommendation:

> *Ye have heard that it was said by them of old time, thou shalt not commit adultery: But I say unto you, that whosoever looketh on a woman to lust after her hath committed adultery with her already in his heart.*
>
> *And if thy right eye offends thee, pluck it out, and cast it from thee: for it is profitable for thee that one of thy members should perish, and not that thy whole body should be cast into hellAnd if thy right hand offends thee, cut it off, and cast it from thee: for it is profitable for thee that one of thy members should perish, and not that thy whole body should be cast into hell.*
>
> **MATTHEW 5:27–30**

How then can the believer escape this impending doom? How can we avoid this demonic magnet that is pulling so many people down the pathway of hell? Those are the things discussed in this book.

Nothing will ruin your testimony more than sexual indiscretions.

God has breathed on this book for your sake. In this material, I 'throw' light on lust as a concept from a holistic point of view but more attention is drawn to the lust for foreplay and sexual intercourse, providing verified biblical principles to overcome same. It is an inspired work, totally orchestrated by the Holy Spirit as a vehicle to saving millions that are heading towards eternal damnation. Yet the principles enunciated here are so practical that you cannot miss it.

This book is for all who desire to live like true children of God. I strongly encourage you therefore to study and meditate on the contents with an open heart and allow God to speak to your heart. You will be glad you did!

Timothy Adebayo

Timothy Adebayo

CHAPTER **ONE**

UNFOLDING THE CONCEPT OF LUST

"Lust begins with a sensation." — Mason Cooley

"Variety and multiplicity are the two most powerful vehicles of lust." —Marquis de Sade

"You have heard that it was said to those of old, 'You shall not commit adultery.' But I say to you that whoever looks at a woman to lust for her has already committed adultery with her in his heart." — Jesus Christ

My Personal Experience

When I was much younger, during my teenage years, any time I came across the word ***lust***, my mind would quickly interpret it as illegitimate sexual or inordinate affection for opposite gender. I assumed that lust is all about wrong sexual desires towards a lady. As I was growing up, I began to notice some 'unique' brothers who had zero interest on females. If someone around them should raise an issue as touching ladies, these "brothers" will suddenly become furious and yell at the person. They would say, "Please, can we discuss something more reasonable?" All their thoughts are centered on how to make 'good' cash and build a career. They become uncomfortable at any discussion relating to male and female emotions or relationship. They are not romantic at all.

I remember Brother Femi, a Christian brother who came from a wretched background, seriously took offence when another friend suggested that "Sister" Florence was interested in him. He showed an alarm that caught everybody by surprise so much so that a story started making the rounds to the effect that he had health challenges that restricted him from love- making. But truth is, he had no health challenge; he was only deeply uninterested in anything emotional or sensual.

I equally observed same attitude in some "sisters" as well: all they care about is cosmetics and fashion, hunting for the latest designer wears, up and down. They are career women and all that bothers them is the public opinion about their outfit and appearance. They are athletes in the rat race to wear dresses that are in vogue to oppress others.

One could be tempted to assume that God created these kinds of brothers and sisters without sexual feelings. Many of such ladies parade themselves in unapproachable manners, unlike their counterparts or friends who run after "brothers" as the hypnotized would do. Some of the brothers in this category barely interact with the sisters and if they do, it is usually from a distance; others do not even have a lady- friend.

Then, I began to ask myself questions: “Does it mean that these set of ‘brothers’ and ‘sisters’ are already free from lust from their mothers' womb?”

As I continued to study the word of God as a young boy and became more knowledgeable, I realized that lust is actually not limited to sexual desires. I also remember one of my high school classmates who was notorious for pilferage and gambling but had no interest for young girls in the school. Even when they want to flock around him because of how he lavished money, he was so unfriendly that most girls related with him from afar and thought of him as arrogant. He was simply in his own world. All that bothered him was how to get cash and how to drink himself to stupor.

I become worried when I see pastors counseling mature single brothers who are old enough to be married on how to confidently approach a lady for a life partner. They would seem to be 'blushing'; they have focused on their careers without any plans to settle down and build a home. It is obvious that being lustfully attracted to an opposite gender is the least of their worries.

As a youth pastor, I do notice same in some sisters as well.

In John 6:8-12, a woman gently rubbed an expensive precious oil in the alabaster box on Jesus’ feet. Some folks around could have thought of the pleasurable feelings of a woman gently rubbing expensive oil and kissing one's feet and quietly wished and imagined in their hearts that their feet were the ones being gently rubbed and kissed.

However, all of these did not appeal to Judas. He was only after the cash. He knew how much exactly it has been sold in the market. He could not hesitate to cry out:

> *"Then saith one of his disciples, Judas Iscariot, Simon's son, which should betray him, why was not this ointment sold for three hundred pence, and given to the poor?*
>
> *This he said, not that he cared for the poor; but because he was a thief, and had the bag, and bare what was put therein."*
>
> **JOHN 6:10-12.**

The lust for mammon was more dominant in Judas than any other. He had no business getting infatuated with any woman. All he lusted after was the cash. No wonder he did not think twice before betraying his Master for thirty pieces of silver coins.

As for Gehazi, it was lust for materialism. How sad it is to remember that it led him to inherit leprosy, not just for himself but also for his unborn descendants.

It is worthy of note that what people lust after is personal to them and cannot be generalized.

The Possessive Nature of Lusts

But every man is tempted, when he is drawn away of his own lust, and enticed."
JAMES 1:14

...his own lust.

From the above text, it is very clear why different persons lust after different things. No one is drawn away after the lust of another but his own. Lust is any strong desire; it is a desire for something that God has forbidden, not necessarily sexual.

Lustful thoughts produce lustful actions, and lust acted upon always leads to devastation. In Matthew 5:27-28, Jesus said that the people have heard that the accepted standard was adultery, but that was not God's line. God set the standard at lust!

When you lust in your heart, you cross the line. Lust involves a choice and an act of the will. To a certain extent it is a conscious decision to pursue the desirable object instead of simply allowing it to pass on. It is a willingness to give in to the natural impulse within and get possessed by same.

Every act of disobedience, social vices and crime in the society is traceable to unbridled lusts locked up inside individuals:

> *"From whence come wars and fighting among you? come they not hence, even of your lusts that war in your members?"*
>
> **JAMES 4:1**

Also, corruption-the deadly devourer found its route into our society through lusts:

> *"Whereby are given unto us exceeding great and precious promises: that by these ye might be partakers of the divine nature, having escaped the corruption that is in the world through lust."*
>
> **I PETER 1:4**

Securing victory over lust is not what you can casually handle. You must be deliberate about it, lest it becomes a clog in the wheel of your progress.

The Bible makes it clear that there is such a thing as personal self-control. That's the good news here. A man can learn to allow such sensory stimuli to bounce off him without the stimuli taking root in his mind and heart. This will be explicitly dealt with in the subsequent chapters.

The Peculiar Nature of Lusts

> *"Flee also youthful lusts: but follow righteousness, faith, charity, peace, with them that call on the Lord out of a pure heart."*
>
> **2 TIMOTHY 2:22**

It is highly imperative for us to know that what appeals to young people does not always appeal to the old folks and there are certain lusts that have their tight grip on you only when you are young. The Devil flashes peculiar things to young people only and does all he can to get the undisciplined youth lust after them so he sifts them as wheat. After all, a wasted youth is most likely to be a useless adult. The Devil is aware that certain things are appealing to you as a young person. He knows that this is the time of foundation-laying. He is fully aware that permanence, even of your physical features only begin now that you're a youth. You are coming to a stage where whatever is formed within you is permanent; it is not likely to change again. He also knows that all that will become of your future and destiny is rooted in your youth. The time of youth is a time of expression, so what entices young people is quite peculiar.

Apostle Paul when admonishing the young man Timothy, instructed him to flee **youthful lusts**; not just ***lusts*** but **youthful ones,** owing to the fact that brother Timothy was a youth.

Have you taken time to observe old men and women; not many things move them. Even when you preach to these people, their response is quite different.

People often say, *"Old people respond differently to issues because almost everything you say only reminds them of their past. Most of their years are already behind. They have not much to look forward to. When you preach to the old people, you only remind them of where they are coming from and only help them to see where they can correct whatever remains before they go to sleep in death."*

Many old people are also in the grip of one lust or the other; the lust for vengeance is much stronger in old people than it is in young people. Also, there are certain lusts that mostly find expression in young people.

When you become old, it does not take much effort to do the correct things. Whether you repent or not, when you are old, certain behaviors will leave you. Your zeal and interest in them gradually dissipate. And even when you do not want to leave them, they will eventually leave you.

For instance, it is only when you are a young person that you can comfortably catwalk up and down the street with a high heeled shoe. When you become old, your legs will no longer find it funny with such shoes. There are many old men who could not but take alcohol when they were young; and as a result, they have got their liver damaged. No need to preach long sermon to them again. Whenever they sip little alcohol, it hurts them badly. Therefore, the peculiarity of lust varies from one age group, culture, environment and way of upbringing to the other.

The Diverse Nature of Lusts

> *"For we ourselves also were sometimes foolish, disobedient, deceived, serving divers lusts and pleasures,*

living in malice and envy, hateful, and hating one another."
TITUS 3:3

The diverse nature of lusts calls for a wider view rather than being myopic and relating it only to inordinate sexual affections.

Paul while charging Timothy instructed the young minister to flee from youthful **'lusts'**, not **'lust'** in 2 Timothy 2:22. Do you notice the plurality? Apostle Paul was much aware that as a young man or woman you might have more than one lust to deal with. You need divine wisdom to deal with every area of lust in your life. Anyone you ignore might be your pitfall overtime.

Individuals get tempted after their own lusts. While some lust after power and position, fashion and extravagant lifestyle, others lust after early independence, ungodly fame and unhealthy wealth, violence and vengeance etc. This explains the diverse nature of lust.

The Conflicting Nature of Lusts

"Dearly beloved, I beseech you as strangers and pilgrims, abstain from fleshly lusts, <u>which war against the soul;</u>"
I PETER 2:11

Everyone in the grip of lust have daily battles to contend with in his or her life. It is an internal battle that may not be easily suspected from the outside. Many so-called Christians could not understand while this battle lingers even after years of being a professing Christian. Pastors, fellowship and group leaders cry in secret after realizing they have acted on the dictates of lust. The desire of the Devil is to see you acting lustfully so that he can stand a chance to claim your soul. He knows that it is written that the soul that sinneth shall die. That is why he flashes appealing things to you for enticement. It is indeed a war against the soul!

In Matthew 4:19, Jesus said that lust is capable of choking the word of God in a man's heart and make it unfruitful; that is the reason why you return to your vomit after that powerful message from that powerful preacher.

Lust can go any length to make God's Word unfruitful in your life. Apostle Paul stated that lust leads to all kinds of uncleanness in Rom 1:24.

Lust sinks men into destruction and perdition; Uncle Achan would explain this better:

> *"And Achan answered Joshua, and said, Indeed I have sinned against the LORD God of Israel, and thus and thus have I done: When I saw among the spoils a goodly Babylonish garment, and two hundred shekels of silver, and a wedge of gold of fifty shekels weight, then I coveted them, and took them; and behold, they are hid in the earth in the midst of my tent, and the silver under it. And Joshua said, why hast thou troubled us? the LORD shall trouble thee this day. And all Israel stoned him with stones, and burned them with fire, after they had stoned them with stones."*

The end result of lust is clearly stated in the word of God; "***Then when lust hath conceived, it bringeth forth sin: and sin, when it is finished, bringeth forth death.***" (James 1:15). To say lust is deadly is not an exaggeration and that God is at variance with lust and as such does not respond to any request based on lust no matter how needful the request might be is clear from James 4:3.

There is a need for you to do a personal x-ray of your heart and expose yourself to yourself with strong determination to deal with that lust before it exposes you to the world and conquers your soul.

Lust has a way of quietly accompanying a man to the peak of his success only to disgrace him and make a fool out of him.

Man of God, don't you think it is high time you cried to the Lord like Peter before you sink and stink in the ocean of lust?

Young brother and sister, this is not the time to be a professional or an expert in hiding this weak point that is patiently journeying with you only to show up and finish you at the edge of breakthrough. You must be deliberate about it now!

I know quite well that there are all kinds of lusts in humans; however, this book is written to address the lust specifically and explicitly for foreplay and sexual intercourse.

In the Greek, the word usually used for lust is "epithymia". This Greek word denotes any strong desire directed towards an object.

In addition, there are three other Greek words that express the word "lust", namely "pathos" (Romans 1 :26; Colossians 3:5, and I Thessalonians 4:5); “Orexis” (Romans 1:27) and “pleonexia" (Ephesians 4:19). These three words express "lust" in terms of *sexual desires*.

In most Bible verses, "lust" is used in a strongly negative sense. Almost all such passages deal with sexual desire stimulated by the sin nature- a desire that seeks to possess and use persons who are not rightly objects of desire.

We must be careful not to suggest that sexual desire itself is wrong. In marriage, sexual desire for one's spouse is good indeed.

CHAPTER **TWO**

THE LUST FOR FOREPLAY AND SEXUAL INTERCOURSE

We will begin by defining some key words here:

✓ ***Foreplay***

According to Wikipedia, *"Foreplay is a set of emotionally and physically intimate acts between two or more people meant to create sexual arousal and desire for sexual activity."*

Oxford Advanced Learner's Dictionary defines it as *"sexual activity, such as touching the sexual organs and kissing, that takes place before sex."*

It is broadly defined as any sexual activity capable of leading up to sex, foreplay can include everything from kissing to massage to, yes, oral sex. Basically, it is anything that turns you and your partner on before you begin having sex.

✓ ***Sexual Intercourse***

Oxford defines it as *"sexual contact between individuals involving penetration, especially the insertion of a man's erect penis into a woman's vagina, typically culminating in orgasm and the ejaculation of semen."*

Sexual intercourse according to Wikipedia, is defined as *"sexual activity typically involving the insertion and thrusting of the penis into the vagina for sexual pleasure, reproduction, or both."*

✓ *Love versus Lust For Sexual Activity*

There is actually a thin line between love and lust. Let me emphasize that foreplay and sexual intercourse within the confinement of marriage between a mature male and female under a divine or human law, culture and procedures is seen as an expression of love.

On the contrary, any form of foreplay and sexual intercourse or any desire for it, between two unmarried partners either of same gender or opposite, or as an extra marital affair is an expression of lust and infatuation.

This book focuses on this nature of lust and how to secure victory over it. You must know that the guilt for foreplay and sexual intercourse is not actually the act of it, but the untamed desire or lust for it;

> *"But I say unto you, that whosoever looketh on a woman to lust after her hath committed adultery with her already in his heart."*
> **Matt 5:28** NKJV

This translation of the Bible makes it a bit clearer:

"But I tell you that whoever looks at a woman and cherishes lustful thoughts has already in his heart become guilty with regard to her."

WEYMOUTH NEW TESTAMENT VERSION

It is also imperative to know that it is not only males that lust. Females do lust as well and are guilty of same.

The wife of Potipher lusted daily after Joseph. It was lust for what she should not have but it nearly crippled Joseph's destiny:

And it came to pass after these things, that his master's wife cast her eyes upon Joseph; and she said, Lie with me.

But he refused, and said unto his master's wife, Behold, my master wotteth not what is with me in the house, and he hath committed all that he hath to my hand;

There is none greater in this house than I; neither hath he kept back anything from me but thee because thou art his wife: how then can I do this great wickedness, and sin against God?

And it came to pass, as she spake to Joseph day by day, that he hearkened not unto her, to lie by her, or to be with her.

And it also came to pass about this time, that Joseph went into the to do his business; and there was none of the men of the house there within.

And she caught him by his garment, saying, Lie with me: and he left his garment in her hand, and fled, and got him out.

And it came to pass, when she saw that he had left his garment in her hand, and was fled forth,

That she called unto the men of her house, and spake unto them, saying, See, he hath brought in a Hebrew unto us to mock us; he came in unto me to lie with me, and I cried with a loud voice:

And it came to pass, when he heard that I lifted up my voice and cried, that he left his garment with me, and fled, and got him out.

And she laid up his garment by her, until his lord came home. And she spake unto him according to these words, saying, The Hebrew servant, which thou hast brought unto us, came in unto me to mock me:

And it came to pass, as I lifted up my voice and cried, that he left his garment with me, and fled out.

And it came to pass, when his master heard the words of his wife, which she spake unto him, saying, after this manner did thy servant to me; that his wrath was kindled.

And Joseph's master took him, and put him into the prison, a place where the king's prisoners were bound and he was there in the prison.

Genesis 39:7-20

Just as a man can lust after a woman, so can a woman lust after a man. Bible historians tell us that Joseph was so handsome that he became the toast of so many women.

Beauty strikes the men as the women. Joseph was handsome and wellshaped and developed in body. (The same Hebrew expressions used of him were also used of Rachel; Genesis 29:17) His beauty was celebrated all over the East. Persian poets and the 12th Chapter of the Koran speak of his beauty as perfect.

Tradition says that Zuleekha, Potipher's wife, was at first the most virtuous of women, but when she saw him, she was so affected that she lost all self- control and became a slave to her passion. On one occasion, she supposedly made a dinner inviting 40 of the most beautiful women of Egypt who, when they saw Joseph, were so moved with admiration that they exclaimed with one accord that he must be an angel.

So, when lust driven fellows tell you that you are an Angel, it won't be the first-time lust is speaking!

The cycle of disobedience is in succession, beginning from the desires of the object of sin, which is lust, to the act, and subsequently to its consequences.

> *"But I-- I say to you, that everyone who is looking on a woman to desire her, did already commit adultery with her in his heart. Everyone is tempted by his own desires as they lure him away and trap him. desire becomes*

pregnant and gives birth to sin. When sin grows up, it gives birth to death."
MATT 5:28, JAMES 1:14-15 (YLT & GWT)

PRINCIPLES

Whenever principles are in place and duly followed, results are inevitable. You must understand that principles are like keys that can unlock doors irrespective of whoever is holding it. They are provable steps that guarantee a definite outcome if taken. As you begin to apply the biblical principles shared in this book, expect a great turnaround in your relationship.

Remember Amnon, the son of David the king. He made a mess of his life and died prematurely due to this unbridled lust. Anybody could have been in Amnon's shoe, struggling to let go of the impulse and desires of the flesh. Many have messed up their Christian faith and defiled their bodies due to infatuation towards a brother or sister:

"Some time passed. David's son Absalom had a beautiful sister namedTamar, and David's son Amnon was infatuated with her."
2 SAMUEL 13:1

Merriam Webster dictionary defines infatuation as *"a short-lived feeling of foolish or obsessively strong love for, admiration for, or interest in someone or something: a strong and unreasoning attachment."*

The young man Amnon also struggled with this infatuation like many of us until he became weak and subjected himself to the grip of the merciless monster called Mr. LUST who brought a sudden end upon Amnon's life as a consequence of his action.

Amnon is not alone in this mad pursuit of the forbidden.

There is a case of Mr. Gbenga who was obsessed with a damsel that was posted to his office, Sylvia. She was very attractive; in fact, almost irresistible. It began to affect his performance at work as he could no longer concentrate on his duties.

Weeks turned into months and his desire grew exponentially. One day, Satan gave him an idea. He organised "armed robbers" to rob her house so that he can have the time and opportunity to rape her. Everything went according to plan but when he forcefully pushed her down to rape her, the mask he used slightly pulled aside and she recognised him. Just at that moment, there was a bang by the estate patrol team and the "armed robbers" made feeble attempts to escape. Being undressed, Gbenga could not move as fast as others and he was subsequently arrested. His confession under torture shook the community as Gbenga had all along been held in high esteem.

Hear this: are you also in the grip of this monster? Or you are living a frustrated life after several attempts to be free but all to no avail? Have you had a similar strong infatuation towards an opposite gender like Amnon or Potipher's wife and you could not control your sexual urge until you had a sexual romantic experience with that brother or sister which eventually led to that sexual intercourse and now you regretted doing it? Maybe you are a lesbian or gay and you have been looking for an escape route from the grip of this lust? Or you have to been eaten up with secret masturbation and longing for a deliverance? Are you in a relationship and you find it difficult to make it sacred and sex free? Or you are even married but the lust for foreplay and sexual intercourse keeps making you to break your marriage vows?

I have good news for you all. You are coming out of that ugly experience this day! This book is written by the inspiration of God to equip you with the right knowledge and empower you for a victorious living over this lust.

My brother and sister, if you will truly secure a lasting victory over this lust, the ball is in your court. You have a vital role to play just as God has His own part to play as well. These roles are buried in the eight biblical principles that are explained in this book.

The character study on Amnon's sexual life, king David's firstborn and other relevant personalities holds for us the eight principles God will have us learn. We will be taking it bit by bit but here is the full story:

> *Some time passed. David's son Absalom had a beautiful sister named Tamar and David's son Amnon was infatuated with her.*

Amnon was frustrated to the point of making himself sick over his sister Tamar because she was a virgin, but it seemed impossible to do anything to her.

Amnon had a friend named Jonadab, a son of David's brother Shimeah. Jonadab was a very shrewd man,

and he asked Amnon, "Why are you, the king's son, so miserable every morning? Won't you tell me?"

Amnon replied, "I'm in love with Tamar, my brother Absalom's sister." Jonadab said to him, "Lie down on your bed and pretend you're sick.

When your father comes to see you, say to him, 'Please let my sister Tamar come and give me something to eat. Let her prepare a meal in my presence so I can watch and eat from her hand."

So Amnon lay down and pretended to be sick. When the king came to see him, Amnon said to him, "Please let my sister Tamar come and make a couple of cakes in my presence so I can eat from her hand."

David sent word to Tamar at the palace: "Please go to your brother Amnon's house and prepare a meal for him."

Then Tamar went to his house while Amnon was lying down. She took dough, kneaded it, made cakes in his presence, and baked them.

She brought the pan and set it down in front of him, but he refused to eat. Amnon said, "Everyone leave me!" And everyone left him.

"Bring the meal to the bedroom," Amnon told Tamar, "so I can eat from your hand." Tamar took the cakes she had made and went to her brother Amnon's bedroom.

When she brought them to him to eat, he grabbed her and said, "Come sleep with me, my sister!"

"Don't, my brother!" she cried. "Don't disgrace me, for such a thing should never be done in Israel. Do not commit this outrage!

Where could I ever go with my humiliation? And you — you would be like one of the outrageous fools in Israel! Please, speak to the king, for he won't keep me from you."

But he refused to listen to her, and because he was stronger than she was, he disgraced her by raping her.

So Amnon hated Tamar with such intensity that the hatred he hated her with was greater than the love he had loved her with. "Get out of here!" he said.

"No," she cried, "sending me away is much worse than the great wrong you've already done to me!" But he refused to listen to her.

Instead, he called to the servant who waited on him: "Get this away from me, throw her out, and bolt the door behind her!"

Amnon's servant threw her out and bolted the door behind her. Now Tamar was wearing a long-sleeved garment because this is what the king's virgin daughters wore. Tamar put ashes on her head and tore the long-sleeved garment she was wearing. She put her hand on her head and went away crying out.

Two years later, Absalom's sheepshearers were at Baal-hazor near Ephraim, and Absalom invited all the king's sons. Then he went to the king and said, "Your servant has just hired sheepshearers. Will the king and his servants please come with your servant?"

The king replied to Absalom, "No, my son, we should not all go, or we would be a burden to you." Although Absalom urged him, he was not willing to go, though he did bless him.

"If not," Absalom said, "please let my brother Amnon go with us." The king asked him, "Why should he go with you?" But Absalom urged him, so he sent Amnon and all the king's sons.

Now Absalom commanded his young men, "Watch Amnon until he is in a good mood from the wine. When I order you to strike Amnon, then kill him. Do not be afraid. Am I not the one who has commanded you? Be strong and valiant!"

So Absalom's young men did to Amnon just as Absalom had commanded. Then all the rest of the king's sons got up, and each fled on his mule.

While they were on the way, a report reached David: "Absalom struck down all the king's sons; not even one of them survived!"

In response the king stood up, tore his clothes, and lay down on the ground, and all his servants stood by with their clothes torn.

But Jonadab, son of David's brother Shimeah, spoke up: "My lord must not think they have killed all the young men, the king's sons, because only Amnon is dead. In fact, Absalom has planned this ever since the day Amnon disgraced his sister Tamar.

So now, my lord the king, do not take seriously the report that says all the king's sons are dead. Only Amnon is dead."

2 SAMUEL 13 (CHRISTIAN STANDARD BIBLE)

CHAPTER **THREE**

Principle I: DO NOT PROVIDE A CONDUCIVE PLACE FOR THE FLESH

"Bring the meal to the bedroom," Amnon told Tamar, "so I can eat from your hand." Tamar took the cakes she had made and went to her brother Amnon's bedroom. (v. 10)

One of the eight powerful principles of overcoming this nature of lust is to deprive oneself from providing a conducive place, location and environment for the flesh to thrive. Amnon was unable to express his infatuation until he drove out everyone except Tamar in verse nine of the chapter and instructed her to bring the meal to his bedroom.

Why the bedroom? This is an attempt to create a conducive atmosphere to satisfy his sexual gratification. Amnon ensured he was left alone with Tamar behind closed door.

It is very unfortunate how many young people find themselves in sexual mess continuously but still do not do anything to help themselves by applying this simple but vital principle.

Believe me, often time, the flesh needs a conducive place to manifest its desires. Most of the time, foreplay and sexual intercourse are most likely to be behind closed doors, spread curtains, locked cars, quite environment, hidden and unsuspected places, dark corners at late night and out of sight locations etc.

This is simply because the flesh often demands for a hideout to manifest fully and freely. If Amnon had allowed the bodyguards and others to stay, he could have suppressed that desire on the said day. Unfortunately, he created a conducive atmosphere for the act.

While in school, Mr. Emmanuel was the Christian Union fellowship President. He had an impeccable testimony that he feared God and eschewed evil. After his graduation and youth service, he started working in a central part of Lagos. As his work entailed distributing drinks to several distributors, he was always on the move.

Late one evening, tired and seriously exhausted from work, he came into view with a lady, one of his converts while in school. They were excited to re- connect.

They exchanged phone numbers and expressed a wish to see each other soon again, more so as their houses were not so far apart. Smiles played on their lips as they parted.

That same weekend, Sister Anthonia came "visiting".

As he had taught while in school, Mr. Emmanuel opened his door ajar and also opened his windows. Anthonia became very uncomfortable. She protested but Emmanuel did not yield. After a while, from nowhere, it started to rain. It was getting late but it would be unfair to ask a lady to head out under the rain. He thought of what to do but his mind came unstuck. Just at that time, Anthonia started getting ready to sleep over, as if she had pre-planned the whole thing. The angrier Emmanuel became, the more she disarmed him with her subtle smiles.

To cut the long story short, she slept over that night but none of them blinked an eye. Neither Emmanuel nor Anthonia enjoyed any moment of sleep. Why? One was a protagonist, pushing for sexual adventure; the other was the antagonist resisting by all necessary means. At the end, both were weary in the morning. It was more than a fight, and that was the last time that both met.

Take this counsel sister: avoid being alone with brothers behind closed doors or creating any conducive environment that can aid the flesh to raise its ugly head.

I will not forget the day a young lady cried to me for help. I told her to stop crying and asked what the matter was. She left her house the previous night to attend a youth vigil at the church headquarters quite far away from her residence. She arrived early, so she decided to visit brother James who happened to be the youth coordinator. Brother

James stayed alone around the vicinity with the intention that they would both leave for the vigil at the time of commencement. Unknown to her, brother James has been struggling with untamed sexual lifestyle which I was very much aware of. It was just thirty minutes to the time they intended to leave that this unusual rain began and it poured heavily for about four hours and so she got trapped.

The rain subsided at midnight. It was just a single room apartment. Doors and windows were locked and there was power outage. What a good atmosphere for the flesh to thrive? She started getting cold, requested for a blanket and as brother James pampered her gently, one thing led to the other and there was an intercourse. She rose up very early and sneaked out of the compound to my place weeping profusely. She became restless due to guilty conscience.

Beloved, being born again does not terminate our emotions, rather it places us in control of it. Brother, one of the nuggets of wisdom you must employ to escape sexual pitfalls in your journey is to avoid being alone with that sister where you can easily lose your guard.

I beseech you to learn from this foolish young man:

> *Once I was looking out the window of my house, And I saw many inexperienced young men but noticed one foolish fellow in particular.*

He was walking along the street near the corner where a certain woman lived. He was passing near her house.

In the evening after it was dark. And then she met him; she was dressed like a prostitute and was making plans. She was a bold and shameless woman who always walked the streets. Or stood waiting at a corner, sometimes in the streets, sometimes in the marketplace.

She threw her arms around the young man, kissed him, looked him straight in the eye, and said, "I made my offerings today and have the meat from the sacrifices.

So I came out looking for you. I wanted to find you, and here you are! I've covered my bed with sheets of colored linen from Egypt. I've perfumed it with myrrh, aloes, and cinnamon. Come on! Let's make love all night long. We'll be happy in each other's arms. My husband isn't at home. He's on a long trip. He took plenty of money with him and won't be back for two weeks."

So she tempted him with her charms, and he gave in to her smooth talk. Suddenly he was going with her like an ox on the way to be slaughtered, like a deer prancing into a trap. Where an arrow would pierce its heart. He was like a bird going into a net—he did not know that his life was in danger. Now then, sons, listen to me. Pay attention to what I say. Do not let such a woman win your heart; don't go wandering after her. She has been the ruin of many men and caused the death of too many to count.

If you go to her house, you are on the way to the world of the dead. It is a shortcut to death.
PROVERBS 7:6-27

Pay close attention to verses 9 and 27.

"Brother" Chidi was admitted to study Theatre Arts in the University of Calabar. While there, he continued his martial arts routine which he started in the primary school. Unknown to him, many ladies fell in love with him because they felt he could defend them from cult boys who violate them by force.

One of such girls that fell in love with him is Augusta. Tall, shapely and very irresistible, Augusta was a lady that commanded attention wherever she went. Her long natural hair was the signature tune of her beauty. In fact, two rival cult leaders had been involved in a deadly cult war because both wanted Augusta. But she was not interested in both; it was Chidi that she loved.

Soon rather than later, Chidi noticed her lustful admiration and fell for it. The first week he took her to a hotel to satisfy his lusts, he was attacked and he lost his two phones. Though he beat off the attackers, he also sustained serious wounds.

Two weeks later, his name topped the list of cult boys expelled by the University, even though he was not actually in any cult. He protested his innocence but nobody listened to him.

Chidi got a Vice Chancellor's contract to continuously train the security department of another university. He lasted only two months before the contract was unceremoniously terminated. Why? Chidi had taken to excessive drinking. He was into such a mess that the jealous members of the security department of the university video recorded him staggering while at work and sent the video to the Vice Chancellor who wasted no time in terminating the contract.

Months later, he was invited to go with others to Borno state to rig elections for a candidate. Little did he know that the vehicle they were travelling with had AK 47 hidden inside. They had gone beyond Abuja and were racing towards Borno state when they got accosted by serious policemen on duty. A detailed search was conducted on the car. The other three guys took off, having known that there were weapons. Chidi did not know and by the time he knew, he had been arrested and taken back to Abuja. There he was for several months in an underground cell.

It was in the cell that he finally took stock of his life. He traced all the tragedies that befell him to the week he spent time with the girl, Augusta. Chidi was lucky to have got a second chance from God; not everybody is as lucky as that. Amnon was not that lucky! Chidi provided the occasion for his lust to thrive...in a hotel room! But what happened between them in that hotel room ruined him for so long!

What you are doing behind a closed door may be killing you. Do not create an occasion for sin!

CHAPTER **FOUR**

Principle II: DO NOT PROVIDE A WRONG SHIP FOR THE FLESH

Amnon had a friend named Jonadab, a son of David's brother Shimeah. Jonadab was a very shrewd man, And he asked Amnon, "Why are you, the king's son, so miserable every morning? Won't you tell me?"

Amnon replied, "I'm in love with Tamar, my brother Absalom's sister." Jonadab said to him, "Lie down on your bed and pretend you're sick.

When your father comes to see you, say to him, 'Please let my sister Tamar come and give me something to eat. Let her prepare a meal in my presence so I can watch and eat from her hand."

2 SAM 13:3–5 CHRISTIAN STANDARD BIBLE

A **Ship** is a platform that conveys a company of people following a similar route or heading toward the same destination.

Ship in this regard could be friend- **ship**, relation- **ship**, partner-**ship**, court- **ship**, and even fellow- **ship**.

Unfortunately for Amnon, he entered into a ship with a bad friend. He maintained friendship with Jonadab, a very subtle guy. Despite the fact that Amnon was madly in love with Tamar, he had no idea of how to go about it until he got a wrong counsel from his crafty friend, Jonadab.

Whoever you keep as friend, partner or fellow will either make or mar you. Just like the saying goes, "show me your friend and I will tell you who you are." It doesn't matter how much you intend you keep sexual sanity; as long as you surround yourself with porous and ungodly friends, your sexual purity is mostly unattainable.

People are often like who their friends are. You must break up with anyone who will defile your sexual purity. Avoid friends, relationships and partners who place no value on sexual purity.

Whenever you meet people, one of the first things to do is to find out what their values are. Any brother or sister who preaches premarital or extramarital sex to you is not good for you no matter how good his manifestoes are.

Do not hesitate to change your circle of friends if need be. Any friend or partner who makes you to violate God's standard on sexual purity without any remorse is a trap for your soul.

Evil communication corrupts good manners. Brother Andrew is a deeply committed Christian. He was doing his HND in a State Polytechnic. He had some classmates who derived pleasure in making him look stupid because he would not join them to do all sorts with female students. Even the female students joined in mocking him.

After their last examinations, these students decided to have an all-night sexual orgy. There were bets on which of the guys can take turns on five girls and get them completely overwhelmed. Two of the boys were determined to win the bet and the girls were giggling and ready.

At the middle of the night, those two students who had just finished their final examinations dropped dead. The girls fled the venue of the party. Upon close examination, it was discovered that the boys took pills they bought from "aboki" so that they can last the whole night and win the bet. That is how promising young men lost their lives prematurely.

They had been laughing at Brother Andrew but at long last, Andrew had the better laugh. Avoid friends who love filthy communication, always wanting to arouse you and create sexual urges.

Rape was not a big deal for Jonadab; meanwhile Amnon was a learner. Jonadab showed him the pathway of rape to accomplish his lustful desire, but unknown to Amnon, it was the pathway to his own premature death.

Beloved, be careful of the **ship** you are entering; friendship, relationship, partnership, courtship, even if it is a fellow- **ship**.

Are you already in a wrong friend- **ship**, court- **ship** or relation- **ship**? It is never too late, come out of it now!

> *"Don't let anyone deceive you. Associating with bad people will ruin decent people."*
> **1 COR 15:33** GOD'S WORD TRANSLATION

The Psalmist put it this way: *When sinners entice you, do not consent.*

There are always pressures from our peers that pull us towards doing evil. There are also pressures from the social media, pressures from virtual friends, pressures from the corrupted systems of this world. But God says we have the power to say "No".

He who cannot say no cannot live a righteous life. He who cannot say no cannot fulfil destiny. And he who cannot say no will seriously be pulled down by lust, no matter how high he has gone. Learn to say NO!

CHAPTER **FIVE**

Principle III: DO NOT PROVIDE A LUXURY OF TIME FOR THE FLESH

"And he said unto him, why art thou, being the king's son, lean from day to day? wilt thou not tell me? And Amnon said unto him, I love Tamar, my brother Absalom's sister."

2 SAM 13:4 NKJV

From the above text, do you notice he said, *"from day to day"*? That reveals the amount of time that Amnon committed to lusting after the beautiful Tamar each day.

Personally, I began to wonder, does it mean he had nothing else to do all day? How could he be so idle that the best of his day went into infatuation? There is a common saying that *"an idle mind is the Devil's workshop."*

Christian Standard Bible puts it this way; "***and he asked Amnon, "Why are you, the king's son, so miserable every morning?***"

The morning time is the best time of the day. Your goals are in front of you. Your energy is fresh and your hope for the day is high. No serious businessman, investor or farmer will waste the morning time. But for Amnon, it's a time of infatuation, and every morning at that.

Doctors tell us that sexual erection comes strongest in the morning. So, it is possible to understand that passage from that point of view. We may not know why mornings create such erections but we must not yield to every erection we have. We are not animals; we are human beings with the power of self-control and discretion.

If you will be free from this lust for sexual romance and intercourse, you must ensure to make adequate use of your time daily, so much so that there will be no minutes left for the flesh to engage. Instead of spending that time with ungodly friends, visiting inappropriate places, idle to the point of loneliness, or watching erotic movies, you can channel that same time to a productive enterprise.

You can as well occupy your time with reading Christian literatures, studying Bible and other books along your field of learning, fasting, praying and a seldom retreat.

Let me tell you a secret; nobody gets addicted to anything without committing time to it. If you know anyone who is addicted to a particular habit, find out from him how much time he has committed to that habit or still committing to it. You will be surprised at his response. Just as it takes time to form a habit, it also takes time to get addicted to anything.

Are you addicted to pornographic movies, romance novels, sexual intercourse and lustful thinking? You are simply a victim of what you have been committing your time into.

Do you have any ungodly lifestyle you want to quit? Do you masturbate frequently? Maybe you are addicted to sex chat and sex video call with a sinful partner? Are you a lesbian or gay and you truly desire to be free from this addiction now? It is not as difficult as you think. Stop giving out your time to that habit or that sinful partner and watch yourself obtain self- deliverance. Divert such time to some productive engagements and capacity building. You will only see those addictions leave you without the laying on of hands.

You can make up your mind today and declare now that there is no more time for nonsense going forward. Why watching a movie for two hours or hanging out with a friend for three hours when you cannot kneel in prayers for an hour? Time is life indeed and an abuse of time is an abuse of life.

Listen to this: if the best of your time goes into things that promote the desires of the flesh, you are in for a big trouble! It is a sign of foolishness when one begins to invest time that is meant for business, spirituality and mental capacity building into love affairs. Everything has it's own rightful time.

'Hate' is not totally a bad word. It depends on the context or application.

You must hate nonsense!

Hate premarital sex!

Hate illegitimate foreplay and extra marital sex.

If you spend time loving what you ought to hate, it is a gross abuse of the irreplaceable time. Effective time management is one of the pathways to overcoming the lust for foreplay and sexual intercourse.

To ever thing there is a season, and a time to every purpose under the heaven:

A time to be born, and a time to die; a time to plant, and a time to pluck up that which is planted;

[8] A time to love, and a time to hate;
ECCLESIASTES 3:1–2, 8a

Why did David fall? He was not where he was supposed to be. While others were at war, he was busy looking at a married woman who was bathing.

And it came to pass, after the year was expired, at the time when kings go forth to battle, that David sent Joab, and his servants with him, and all Israel; and they destroyed the children of Ammon, and besieged Rabbah. But David tarried still at Jerusalem.

And it came to pass in an eveningtide, that David arose from off his bed, and walked upon the roof of the king's house: and from the roof he saw a woman washing herself; and the woman was very beautiful to look upon.

And David sent and enquired after the woman. And one said, Is not this Bathsheba, the daughter of Eliam, the wife of Uriah the Hittite?

And David sent messengers and took her; and she came in unto him, and he lay with her; for she was purified from her uncleanness: and she returned unto her house.

2 Samuel 11:1-4

While kings went to war, David was at home looking for a woman to sleep with! Yet he had wives at this time. He made provision for the flesh, to fulfil the lusts thereof.

When Jesus talked of cutting our hands rather than lusting or plucking out our eyes, the first thing to do is to make sure that you make no provision for the flesh to fulfil its lusts.

Stop indulging in chats that are erotic. It would never help you.

CHAPTER SIX

Principle IV: DO NOT PROVIDE AN UNGUARDED EYE FOR THE FLESH

Some time passed. David's son Absalom had a beautiful sister named Tamar, and David's son Amnon was infatuated with her. 2 Sam 13:1 Christian Standard Bible

Love not the world, neither the things that are in the world. If any man loves the world, the love of the Father is not in him. For all that is in the world, the lust of the flesh, and the lust of the eyes, and the pride of life, is not of the Father, but is of the world.

And the world passeth away, and the lust thereof: but he that doeth the will of God abideth forever.

1 JOHN 2:15-17

The Bible is clear: *all that is in the world is lust of the flesh, lust of the eye and pride of life.* In this Chapter, we shall focus on the lust of the eyes. What does the lust of the eye mean? To answer this question from our key passage, we go to the first passage quoted in this Chapter.

The Bible did not keep us in the dark concerning the genesis of Amnon's fall which eventually led to his untimely death. The

Scriptures reveal the beginning of the problem by letting us know that Tamar was a very beautiful young lady and Amnon could not subdue his sexual gratification each time he saw her beauty with his unguarded eyes.

Obviously, one of the things that got Amnon infatuated with Tamar was her notable beauty. Like the saying goes, *"beauty is in the eyes of the beholder*".

Real beauty is not limited to the facial look of a lady. Beauty is more of the entire body structure and shape than just a facial look. The physique of a lady, the shape of her face, the size of her breast, the accurate hip size, average butt size, flat tummy, height, including the shape of the legs are what determine how a lady's physical beauty is rated in the modeling industry, among others.

Amnon was carried away by one or more of the aforementioned physical qualities. Brother, which of these above-mentioned qualities of a lady easily entices or appeals to your unguarded eyes and has made you to fall into the sin of immorality again and again?

Sister, do you want to be free from this monster called lust, except for your weakness to discipline your eyes from 'falling' for every tall and handsome brother that walks into your life? This is the same weakness that Potipher's wife could not conquer.

Amnon was unable to guard his eyes which eventually made him a prey and a victim. He placed no value on inner beauty which surpasses the external.

Always remember this: what a man focuses upon will soon be the focus of his life. Job understood this principle and he said to himself;

"I made a covenant with my eyes; how then should I look lustfully at a young woman?
JOB 31:1 NEW HEART ENGLISH BIBLE

There is a quote that says, *"What I hear, I forget. What I see I remember."*

Every erotic films and sexual images you constantly watch on your phone is downloaded into your subconscious and will often replay itself without you having to press the play button again. The eye is a powerful gateway that leads to the heart of every individual.

Many people have become victims of their sight. Their inability to control their drive for a beautiful sister or handsome brother says it all. Here are two other examples of men with unguarded eye:

✓ ***DAVID:***

One evening David got up from his bed and strolled around on the roof of the palace. From the roof HE SAW A WOMAN bathing--a very beautiful woman. So David sent someone to inquire about her, and he reported, "This is Bathsheba, daughter of Eliam and wife of Uriah the Hittite." David sent messengers to get her, and when she came to him, he slept with her.
1 SAM 11:2-4a HOLMAN CHRISTIAN STANDARD BIBLE

✓ **SAMSON:**

Samson went to Gaza. There HE SAW A PROSTITUTE and went in to have sex with her.

JUDGES 16:1 NET BIBLE

This was not the first time that Samson would be infatuated.

And Samson went down to Timnath and saw a woman in Timnath of the daughters of the Philistines.

And he came up, and told his father and his mother, and said, I have seen a woman in Timnath of the daughters of the Philistines: now therefore get her for me to wife.

Then his father and his mother said unto him, is there never a woman among the daughters of thy brethren, or among all my people, that thou goest to take a wife of the uncircumcised Philistines? And Samson said unto his father, Get her for me; for she pleaseth me well.

JUDGES 14:1-3

Why Samson was always getting attracted to wrong ladies beats my imagination. He was never interested in getting married to God's people.

Just like many believers today!

In this generation, men are more interested in other criteria than in Christian ladies. They find all sorts of excuses why they are not keen on godly ladies. Some blatantly say they want ladies that can go beyond the ordinary when it comes to sexual activities and hence do not care about the spirituality of the lady. Some even mock ladies who marry pastors because they believe their sexual activities at home would be boring.

They say sexual compatibility is a pre-requisite for a successful marriage — a total fallacy from the pits of hell.

Samson was always attracted to strange women and it was a strange woman that cut short his life. Again, I say, what you love most may be killing you.

If you continue to expose your eyes to sexual images, pornography and half-nude music videos, you are treading on a dangerous path. The story did not end well for David, Samson and Amnon.

An unguarded eye is a tool that the flesh usually uses, in pursuit of its lustful desire. Addiction to porn video can lead to all kinds of immorality like masturbation and frequent sexual urges. Addiction to reading romance novels, and watching sexual comedy and cartoons are ways of providing an unguarded eye for the flesh.

You must discipline your eyes now to avoid being disciplined by your unguarded eyes.

> *But the Philistines took Samson, and put out his eyes, and brought him down to Gaza, and bound him with fetters of brass; and he did grind in the prison house.*
> **JUDGES 16:21 KJV**

When you look at the opposite sex, what do you see? Do you undress her in your mind and proceed to take her to bed?

When Amnon saw Tamar, he saw an object of sex, a tool for sexual gratification. He did not see his half-sister. He did not see the king's daughter. He did not see Absalom's sister. He just saw the tool for gratifying the lusts lurking in his heart.

Again, I ask: when you look at the opposite sex, what do you see?

We must conclude this Chapter by looking at the operational methods of the evil one. Satan uses the same methods most of the time because he finds it very effective.

In the garden of Eden, Satan used the same method on Eve. It is what you see that can tempt you.

> *And when the woman saw that the tree was good for food, and that it was pleasant to the eyes, and a tree to be desired to make one wise, she took of the fruit thereof, and did eat, and gave also unto her husband with her; and he did eat.*
>
> **Genesis 3:6**

Eve saw...

Eve saw that the fruit was good for food! What Eve saw in that garden has kept the world almost in a perpetual mess since then.

We must avoid the lust of the eyes by all means!

What you see can influence whether you operate by faith or by fear. When Peter saw the wind, his faith "evaporated" even though he was with Jesus.

> *But the ship was now in the midst of the sea, tossed with waves: for the wind was contrary.*
>
> *And in the fourth watch of the night Jesus went unto them, walking on the sea.*
>
> *And when the disciples saw him walking on the sea, they were troubled, saying, It is a spirit; and they cried out for fear.*
>
> *But straightway Jesus spake unto them, saying, Be of good cheer; it is I; be not afraid.*
> *And Peter answered him and said, Lord, if it be thou, bid me come unto thee on the water.*
>
> *And he said, Come. And when Peter was come down out of the ship, he walked on the water, to go to Jesus.*
>
> *But when he saw the wind boisterous, he was afraid; and beginning to sink, he cried, saying, Lord, save me.*
>
> *And immediately Jesus stretched forth his hand, and caught him, and said unto him, O thou of little faith, wherefore didst thou doubt?*
>
> **MATTHEW 14:24–31**

Peter saw the wind boisterous!!! He did not sink before then. He had to look away from Jesus and look at the wind before he could sink. His faith took flight because he saw the wrong things.

When you see what you are not supposed to see - the nakedness of the opposite sex- then you will do what you are not supposed to do.

When you see what you are supposed to see, then you will do what you are supposed to do.

Abraham saw the number of stars that God had asked him to count, and faith swelled up within him. What you see determines whether you will operate by faith or by fear.

So, I ask again: What do you see? The author of Hebrews tells us:

> *Looking unto Jesus the author and finisher of our faith; who for the joy that was set before him endured the cross, despising the shame, and is set down at the right hand of the throne of God.*
>
> **HEBREWS 12:2**

CHAPTER **SEVEN**

Principle V: DO NOT PROVIDE A THOUGHT PLATFORM FOR THE FLESH

First, we see, then we think!

And Amnon was so vexed, that he fell sick for his sister Tamar; for she was a virgin; and Amnon thought it hard for him to do anything to her.
2 Sam 13:2 CHRISTIAN STANDARD BIBLE

When you "see" things which you should not see, then you begin to think thoughts which you should not think. The mind often meditates on what it sees. It's easier to refuse to "see" some things than to stop yourself from thinking about them.

It was a philosopher that said we see things as we are! By that he meant that how we interpret what we see is a reflection of what we are. We must hasten to add that William Shakespeare said there is no science to determine what thoughts are going through a mind by looking at the face.

That is how complicated the thought processes are!

If you think long enough you will find solutions to most human problems. If you think long and hard enough, you will find a way to fulfil the lusts that are driving you. So thinking is an integral part of the problem and thinking is also an integral part of the solution.

What does this mean? What you think affects you more than you may be able to admit. Amnon's heart was preoccupied with the thoughts of executing his selfish and lustful passion on Tamar until he thought it hard *to get her.*

One of the greatest havocs that a man can bring upon himself is to provide a thought platform for the flesh to explore. If the flesh can influence your thinking, then your life is at the mercy of its desires.

The word of God admonishes us;

> *"Guard your heart above all else, for it determines the course of your life.*
> **PROVERBS 4:23** NLT

From this Scripture, we are counseled to pay the highest attention and give priority to our hearts where our thoughts are primarily formed, above all else. Without any iota of doubt, your thought life determines the course of your life. That simply means your life is a direct reflection of your thoughts.

Whatever your thoughts are, you must become eventually. Amnon thought of having sex with his own sister and finally he did. The book of Proverbs 23:7a summarizes every man's life with this holistic statement;

"For as he thinketh in his heart, so is he:"
When you think poverty, you remain poor.
When you think small, you remain small.
When you think fear, you live in fear.
When you think wealth, you attract wealth.
When your thoughts are healthy, your life is healthy.
When your thoughts are evil, you exemplify evil. Same for when your thoughts are lustful and immoral, you will eventually live a lustful and immoral life.

Your physical life is simply a report card of your thought life.

You must ensure you do a constant review of your thoughts. Your thoughts are your silent words that later turnout in actions. If you allow your mind to be overwhelmed with sexual and filthy thoughts, you will soon become a victim of such thoughts. This very version of the Bible makes it more clearer; "

> *Be careful how you think; your life is shaped by your thoughts."*
>
> **PROVERBS 4:23** GOOD NEWS BIBLE

It is your thoughts that determine the direction your life will follow. What do you do when you discover that evil thoughts crop up in your heart? Rebuke them. Do not rebuke them silently in your mind: speak it out!

Drown Satan's voice suggesting carnal thoughts by openly and boldly and loudly telling Satan to go behind you. Jesus told Peter, "Satan go behind me!"... And he did so openly! Learn to rebuke strange sexual thoughts that may want to creep into your heart unnoticed. Focus your imagination on things that are beneficial.

Apostle Paul instructed us:

> *"Think about the things of heaven, not the things of earth."*
> **COLOSSIANS 3 :2** NLT

Henceforth, do not entertain evil and satanic thoughts suggesting to you that sexual purity is not sustainable. Every voice whispering to your heart that there is no dignity in keeping your virginity and pressuring you to engage in premarital sex is demonic.

Silence it! Boldly silence it.

Brother, that inner voice that tells you that having sex with a virgin is sweeter and you are now on a virgin hunt is from the Devil; that was the same thought that was used to manipulate Amnon.

Please, do not give room for the thought that springs up harmlessly in your heart but often ends up in masturbation afterwards.

The flesh will do all it can to dominate your thought platform. You must resist it! It is a battle; you have to win!

> *Neither give place to the devil.*

EPHESIANS 4:27

My Sister, if you will consistently overcome the lust for sexual romance and intercourse, then you must learn how to police your mind and cast off every immoral thought striving to initiate a conversation with you;

> *"Casting down imaginations, and every high thing that exalteth itself against the knowledge of God, and bringing into captivity every thought to the obedience of Christ;"*
> **2 CORINTHIANS 10:5**

Brother, you must guard your heart from straying thoughts. You can't be casual about this. You must also be aware that "straying thoughts is the mother of straying eyes and straying feet."

If you cannot control your thoughts, you cannot control your life. If you cannot control your thoughts, you cannot control your destiny.

There are believers who read the romance novels of James Hadley Chase and other books. There are those who spent time watching romance TV plays and movies. There are many today who are addicts of suggestive works. We must learn that we need to constantly purge our minds and hearts of all sorts of suggestive words, images and thoughts. It is a daily battle we cannot afford to lose. Nobody is so spiritual that he may not be tempted. We must therefore push ourselves to the limit by insisting on disinfecting our minds and hearts. If you lose the control of your thoughts, you have lost the control of your life and destiny.

Sometimes we spiritualize our problems when all we need to do is to disinfect our minds. The only effective way to do so is to meditate rather on the word of God and then speak out boldly the word of God to your own mind and heart.

Meditation gives you the power to control your thoughts:

> *[8] This book of the law shall not depart out of thy mouth; but thou shalt meditate therein day and night, that thou mayest observe to do according to all that is written therein: for then thou shalt make thy way prosperous, and then thou shalt have good success.*
>
> **Joshua 1:8**

Moses had this to say:

> *And these words, which I command thee this day, shall be in thine heart:*
>
> *And thou shalt teach them diligently unto thy children, and shalt talk of them when thou sittest in thine house, and when thou walkest by the way, and when thou liest down, and when thou risest up.*
>
> *And thou shalt bind them for a sign upon thine hand, and they shall be as frontlets between thine eyes. And thou shalt write them upon the posts of thy house, and on thy gates.*
>
> **Deuteronomy 6:6–9**

The whole idea behind what Moses was recommending was to control what you see and then control also what you think about.

This is a spiritual law that cannot be broken.

You cannot be feasting your eyes on pornographic materials and yet be hoping to avoid sexual indiscretions; that would be self-deception.

I commit you to the grace of our Lord Jesus Christ and these words on marble for a coordinated and healthy thinking:

> *"Finally, brethren, whatsoever things are true, whatsoever things are honest, whatsoever things are just, whatsoever things are pure, whatsoever things are lovely, whatsoever things are of good report; if there be any virtue, and if there be any praise, think on these things."*
>
> **PHILIPPIANS 4:8**

CHAPTER **EIGHT**

Principle VI: WALK IN THE SPIRIT

So Amnon hated Tamar with such intensity that the hatred he hated her with was greater than the love he had loved her with. "Get out of here!" he said.

"No," she cried, "sending me away is much worse than the great wrong you've already done to me!" But he refused to listen to her.

Instead, he called to the servant who waited on him: "Get this away from me, throw her out, and bolt the door behind her are.

2 SAMUEL 13:15-17

This I say then, walk in the Spirit, and ye shall not fulfil the lust of the flesh.

GALATIANS 5:16

Walking in the Spirit is the pathway of dominion over the flesh. It is very imperative to know that beyond all human efforts and application of carnal principles to overcome lust, the bible gives us a vital and an indispensable instruction in exercising dominion over the flesh and its desires by "walking in the Spirit".

This is where many people are missing it. They use human strength and techniques to combat the human nature without adding the Spirit to the equation. The will of the flesh is compelling on a natural man and our culture, dressing, society, thinking and systems are built to propagate the desires of the flesh. It is only the Spirit of God that has a contrary desire to that of the flesh. Therefore, it is of a paramount importance to walk in the Spirit by having fraternity with the Holy Spirit to silence the voice of the flesh.

> *"For what our human nature wants is opposed to what the Spirit wants, and what the Spirit wants is opposed to what our human nature wants. These two are enemies, and this means that you cannot do what you want to do."*
>
> **GALATIANS 5:17** GNT

It is very obvious that both the Spirit and the flesh have their desires and you are at the mercy of who you yield to. The above Scripture defines the present experience of many people regarding lust and they do not know what to do after applying all known principles to no avail. If you belong to this category, you need to yield more to Holy Spirit and His dynamic power to secure a lasting victory over lust.

This is how the Passion Bible puts it,

> *"As you yield freely and fully to the dynamic life and power of the Holy Spirit, you will abandon the cravings of your self – life."*
> **THE PASSION TRANSLATION**

Your deliverance resides in your continuous yielding to the Spirit. You yield to the Spirit as you engage priesthood. Prayer is that connecting link that opens up your sprit to the influence and governance of the Holy Spirit. There is a level of persistence in prayer and fasting that makes you to lose contacts with the desires the flesh. Even though the flesh is communicating but you will not be able to pick the signal because you are in the Spirit.

There are cases of lusts that demonic spirits are involved. They supply supernatural strength for humans to engage in wild and violent sexual practices. Most harlots, if not all are under the influence of these spirits of Sodom. These Satanic spirits create strong sexual appetite and compel their victims to be involved in sexual immorality.

Oftentimes, there are spirits' influences. The Bible speaks about the spirit of Jezebel. Many persons that often masturbate and are involved in immoral act such as gay practices, lesbianism, incest and bestiality do so under a demonic influence.

The kind of hatred Amnon had for Tamar after the sexual act revealed that he was under an influence. The hatred was unimaginable and inhuman. It looks like a force beyond him was sponsoring the desperation. After he messed up, his eyes cleared and he realized he never wanted her in the first place.

During counseling, I have met with many brothers and sisters who can't explain why they kept falling into immorality after several resolutions and genuine repentance. After committing the act, their eyes would open and they would suddenly develop keen hatred for their sinful partners. They could attest to the fact that they were under a demonic influence beyond their natural selves There are people who hear voices compelling them to such act.

God's desire is sexual purity and He wants you to be free from all forms of demonic influences. Praying in the Spirit, fasting often, confessing Scriptures and living a life of worship are ways of walking in the Spirit. As you begin to make a practice of these things, your desires will gradually align with that of the Holy Spirit and you won't be able to fulfill the desires of the flesh.

There is a need to see fornication beyond an act. It goes deeper than most people realize:

> *What? know ye not that he which is joined to an harlot is one body? for two, saith he, shall be one flesh.*
>
> *But he that is joined unto the Lord is one spirit.*
>
> **1 Corinthians 6:16–17**

He that has intercourse with a harlot has become one with the harlot. A minister of the gospel shared a story that vividly illustrates this deep spiritual truth. A lady, Helen brought her fiancé, Alfred, to the ministry for prayers. Alfred had serious mental issues and was also violent. They prayed for so long and yet there was no result. So, the Senior Pastor felt sufficiently provoked to fast and pray himself. Then God spoke.

The Senior Pastor then called Helen and interviewed her. It was then the truth came out: the mental problems started after she started sleeping with him. In his family, there is no history or case of mental problems but her father, not his, was mad and was actually in the market, naked and violent.

Also, her elder brother died a mad man.

So what must have happened?

We may not have all the answers but what is obvious is, there was a transference of spirits from her to him. She wasn't mad but the spirit of madness was having a stronghold over her family which she had not been delivered from, the spirit was waiting for a good time to manifest. Alfred became a victim through traference during the premarital sex.

So you see, demons cannot be stopped by the use of condoms. You can wear double condoms but it will not stop spirits from moving from one person to the other. Thus, when Paul wrote that, he who has intercourse with a harlot had become one with the harlot, do you not cringe at that thought?

How many demons live inside an average harlot? What if all the demons inside a harlot get transferred to you during intercourse?

The opposite sex that you are "running package" with, do you know how many other people are sexually involved with him or her? What happens if all the demons in him or her get transferred to you?

Can you now begin to understand why after a while, partners begin to acquire new habits, new traits etc.?

We must be very careful whom we have any sexual dealings with. In some other cases, there are divergent spirits involved.

God's admonition for you is to "walk in the Spirit". Learn to tarry in the place of prayer. When prayer becomes your lifestyle, demons and the vessels they possessed won't be comfortable around you. Live a fasted life and watch lustful desires leaving you. The Holy Spirit is always willing to deliver us and help our infirmities if only we will yield to Him.

You have everything it takes to overcome the lust for foreplay and sexual intercourse. You have been bought with a price and your body is the temple of the Holy Spirit.

Beloved, I strongly believe that as you continue to apply these biblical principles, your victory over the lust for foreplay and sexual intercourse is indisputable.

Please, remember these principles and keep them in the deepest part of your heart. Anyone who fell into the sin of lust and sexual intercourse must have broken one or more of these principles. Determine in your heart today to live by these godly principles for a victorious Christian life.

There is a kind of prayer that I find effective in dealing with such issues: "God, I cancel and destroy every relationship, appointment, programme or incident that would bring me in contact with the opposite sex in a wrong way in Jesus Name. I give the Spirit of God all the consent to forcefully stop me from myself if and when I become stubborn and deaf to the promptings of the Spirit of God within me. Lord, deliver me from all inordinate desires of all types with all opposite sex and grant me the grace to live a life of purity and holiness in Jesus Name."

We must conclude this chapter by looking at this Scripture:

> *But without faith it is impossible to please him: for he that cometh to God must believe that he is, and that he is a rewarder of them that diligently seek him.*
> **HEBREWS 11:6**

Oh how I love this: God is! Yes, God is! It did not say God was! It did not say God will be! God is. It's in present continuous tense! God is! It does not matter what happens, God is! It does not matter how ferocious the battle is, God is. It does not matter how many times you have fallen; God is.

Beloved, we must be rest assured and convinced that God is. Right now, God is. No matter what Satan throws our way, God is. So when the lustful ideas and thoughts prop up, God is! So walk in the Spirit and rely on Him to overcome. He said:

> *There hath no temptation taken you but such as is common to man: but God is faithful, who will not suffer you to be tempted above that ye are able; but will with the temptation also make a way to escape, that ye may be able to bear it.*
>
> **1 Corinthians 10:13**

It does not matter what "new" strategies Satan is using: you have God who has promised that you will not be tempted beyond what you are able to handle.

So cheer up beloved. Your God is!

CHAPTER **NINE**

Principle VII: EMBRACE GOD'S PROVISION TO OVERCOME SIN AND ITS LUSTFUL DESIRES

God is aware of every of our weaknesses and challenges and has made a provision for our victory in Christ. Being aware of this provision and exploring it is the total deliverance our lives need.

In the last Chapter we saw that to walk in the spirit is God's panacea for inordinate affections. But how do we achieve this practically in addition to subscribing to a life of prayer and fasting?

> *If a man has a stubborn and rebellious son, which will not obey the voice of his father, or the voice of his mother, and that, when they have chastened him, will not hearken unto them:*
>
> *Then shall his father and his mother lay hold on him, and bring him out unto the elders of his city, and unto the gate of his place;*
>
> *And they shall say unto the elders of his city, This our son is stubborn and rebellious, he will not obey our voice; he is a glutton, and a drunkard. [21] And all the men of his city shall stone him with stones, that he dies:*

so shalt thou put evil away from among you; and all Israel shall hear, and fear.

And if a man has committed a sin worthy of death, and he be to be put to death, and thou hang him on a tree:

His body shall not remain all night upon the tree, but thou shalt in any wise bury him that day; (for he that is hanged is accused of God;) that thy land be not defiled, which the LORD thy God giveth thee for an inheritance.

DEUTERONOMY 21:18-23

You may be wondering what a "rebellious son" has to do with the flesh. Let me make it easier: re- read the passage by replacing "son" with "flesh".

Does that make it clearer?

The flesh is as a stubborn son. The only solution to the flesh is death. You cannot reform the flesh. You cannot amend it. You cannot adjust it to accommodate the Spirit. It has to die. It has to be destroyed. No more, no less.

Paul told of the stubborn nature of the flesh:

For we know that the law is spiritual: but I am carnal, sold under sin.

For that which I do I allow not: for what I would, that do I not; but what I hate, that do I.

If then I do that which I would not, I consent unto the law that it is good.

Now then it is no more I that do it, but sin that dwelleth in me.

For I know that in me (that is, in my flesh,) dwelleth no good thing: for to will is present with me; but how to perform that which is good I find not.

For the good that I would I do not: but the evil which I would not, that I do.

Now if I do that I would not, it is no more I that do it, but sin that dwelleth in me.

I find then a law, that, when I would do good, evil is present with me. [22] For I delight in the law of God after the inward man:

[25] I thank God through Jesus Christ our Lord. So then with the mind I myself serve the law of God; but with the flesh the law of sin.

Romans 7:14-22,25

So we see that the flesh is like a rebellious son who does not listen to the dictates of the owner. What he wants to do, the flesh does not allow him; what he does not want to do, the flesh pushes him to do.

Can you imagine a car in which the driver turns the steering wheel right and the car goes left? That is exactly the imagery. The flesh does not obey the dictates of the Spirit.

Paul went further:

There is therefore now no condemnation to them which are in Christ Jesus, who walk not after the flesh, but after the Spirit.

For the law of the Spirit of life in Christ Jesus hath made me free from the law of sin and death.

For what the law could not do, in that it was weak through the flesh, God sending his own Son in the likeness of sinful flesh, and for sin, condemned sin in the flesh:

That the righteousness of the law might be fulfilled in us, who walk not after the flesh, but after the Spirit.

For they that are after the flesh do mind the things of the flesh; but they that are after the Spirit the things of the Spirit.

For to be carnally minded is death; but to be spiritually minded is life and peace.

Because the carnal mind is enmity against God: for it is not subject to the law of God, neither indeed can be.

So then they that are in the flesh cannot please God.

But ye are not in the flesh, but in the Spirit, if so be that the Spirit of God dwell in you. Now if any man has not the Spirit of Christ, he is none of his.

And if Christ be in you, the body is dead because of sin; but the Spirit is life because of righteousness.

But if the Spirit of him that raised up Jesus from the dead dwell in you, he that raised up Christ from the dead shall also quicken your mortal bodies by his Spirit that dwelleth in you.

Therefore, brethren, we are debtors, not to the flesh, to live after the flesh.

For if ye live after the flesh, ye shall die: but if ye through the Spirit do mortify the deeds of the body, ye shall live.

For as many as are led by the Spirit of God, they are the sons of God.

ROMANS 8:1-14

So we see that the Bible prescription is death to the flesh, same death to the rebellious son!

When we walk in the Spirit, we have no condemnation.

When we walk in the Spirit, we do not fulfil the desires of the flesh.

When we walk in the Spirit, we live and not die! And when we walk in the Spirit, we live as true Sons of God!!

That means we cannot become living testimonies and true manifestations of the Sons of God unless we first die. To live, we have to die first. Except the seed of corn falls to the ground and dies, it abides alone. It is in the resurrected seed that we find fruit that satisfies. In the same way, it is in the resurrected Christian that we find God's fullest blessing.

There is only one person who has complete victory over sin and lust – **a dead man**. A dead man has lost his ability to sin. Until a man is dead, he can never be free from lust.

The word of God says,

> *"For he that is dead is freed from sin."*
> **ROMANS 6:7**

A dead man cannot be tempted with a beautiful naked lady because whoever is dead is free from committing sin. So God's way of setting us free from the power of sin and its lust is to ensure that we are dead and this He accomplished in Christ Jesus as Christ died on our behalf. Thereafter, we are declared dead;

> *"For ye are dead, and your life is hid with Christ in God."*
> **COL 3:3**

The International Standard Version puts it this way, *"For you have died, and your life has been safely guarded by the Messiah in God."*

The most important step to your deliverance is to accept this simple truth – you have died. You died when Christ gave up the ghost on the cross for your sake. Hear me well, you are not dying or going to die. You are dead already. Glory to God. By simply accepting and embracing this gospel truth, you are already securing your victory.

> *"Likewise reckon ye also yourselves to be dead indeed unto sin, but alive unto God through Jesus Christ our Lord."*
>
> **ROMANS 6:11**

What does it mean to reckon? The Greek word for 'reckon' in the above text is 'logizomai' which by interpretation means to account. To "reckon" therefore is to account yourself to be dead. It means to think of yourself as being dead to sin. For instance, when an occasion that should make you lose your temper shows up, you reckon by asking yourself if a dead man can express the bitterness and anger you are about to display. If that is not possible, you then refrain from such uncontrollable anger by also considering yourself to be dead unto sin.

In the same way, you are to resist and cast down every lustful desire, having an understanding that a dead man is free from such desire. Do not allow such desire to find root in your heart. If you must sustain the discipline, you must always think of yourself as being dead unto sin. The more you reckon yourself to be dead, the stronger you are to overcome temptations and lusts. As you continue to embrace God's provision for your deliverance by holding on to your death in Christ and reckoning yourself accordingly, sin and its desire which is lust will keep losing their grip on your life. Hallelujah!

> *"I am crucified with Christ: nevertheless, I live; yet not I, but Christ liveth in me: and the life which I now live*

in the flesh I live by the faith of the Son of God, who loved me, and gave himself for me."
GAL. 2:20

You cannot fight the battles of life with the arms of the flesh. By the arms of the flesh shall no man prevail.

Paul talks about reckoning ourselves dead. You may be young but until you go to the Cross, you are of no value to the kingdom of God.

A final word. We must covet the presence of God. We cannot do anything that has spiritual value without the presence of God. And we cannot become anything or a person of value to God's kingdom without the manifest presence of God in our lives.

A consciousness of the presence of God is an absolute necessity to the life of every believer.

Moses understood this very well:

And Moses said unto the LORD, See, thou sayest unto me, bring up this people: and thou hast not let me know whom thou wilt send with me. Yet thou hast said, I know thee by name, and thou hast also found grace in my sight.

Now therefore, I pray thee, if I have found grace in thy sight, shew me now thy way, that I may know thee, that I may find grace in thy sight:

and consider that this nation is thy people. And he said, My presence shall go with thee, and I will give thee rest.

And he said unto him, If thy presence go not with me, carry us not up hence. For wherein shall it be known here that I and thy people have found grace in thy sight? is it not in that thou goest with us? so shall we be separated, I and thy people, from all the people that are upon the face of the earth.

And the LORD said unto Moses, I will do this thing also that thou hast spoken for thou hast found grace in my sight, and I know thee by name.

And he said, I beseech thee, shew me thy glory. And he said, I will make all my goodness pass before thee, and I will proclaim the name of the LORD before thee; and will be gracious to whom I will be gracious and will shew mercy on whom I will shew mercy.

And he said, Thou canst not see my face: for there shall no man see me, and live. And the LORD said, Behold, there is a place by me, and thou shalt stand upon a rock:

And it shall come to pass, while my glory passeth by, that I will put thee in a clift of the rock, and will cover thee with my hand while I pass by: And I will take away mine hand, and thou shalt see my back parts: but my face shall not be seen.

Exodus 33:12-23

Moses knew that without God's manifest presence, he cannot fulfil his mission on earth. He went to the mountains occasionally to seek

God's face and God thundered many times to authenticate His calling upon his life, but Moses wanted God to always show up and take over.

That same presence of God is what you and I need if we must win the race of life. That same manifest presence of God is what we need if we must shun all youthful vices and live a life of true holiness unto the Lord. Sometime ago, I was in a meeting and the moderator said, " Close your eyes and imagine that God is in our midst".

The presence of God is real; it is not an imagination. If God is present, then He is present and He will show Himself. If God is not present, you may imagine all you want but He will not show Himself.

When Satan pushes you to lock the door as the opposite sex comes near, remember that God is there. When Satan pushes you to undress before a person who is not your spouse, remember that God is there!

When Satan pushes you to go and buy and use condom on a person who is not married to you, remember that God is there! When Satan pushes you to put on a blue film for the amorous arousal of your invitee, remember that God is there!

A song writer said: "You cannot hide it from God. You may cover your sin that nobody may know but you cannot hide it from God."

Nothing will take you away from the grip of lust as fast as the ever-abiding consciousness of the presence of God. That is the panacea that is missing in today's world.

If you want to live a life of victory over lust, cultivate a consciousness of the presence of God. Always know that God is where you are, closer to you than your breath.

CHAPTER **TEN**

Principle VIII: FLEE STILL MEANS FLEE

Flee fornication. Every sin that a man doeth is without the body; but he that committeth fornication sinneth against his own body.

1 CORINTHIANS 6:18

We have been looking at what transpired between Amnon and Tamar. The Bible Chronicler situated this incident as an immediate fallout of the prophecy of Nathan to David, concerning David's indiscretion with Uriah's wife.

In Second Samuel 12:11, Nathan quoted God:

[11] Thus saith the LORD, Behold, I will raise up evil against thee out of thine own house, and I will take thy wives before thine eyes, and give them unto thy neighbour, and he shall lie with thy wives in the sight of this sun.

2 SAMUEL 12:11

So, in fulfilment of this curse, Amnon, David's firstborn conceived an illicit passion for his half-sister. Tamar was his brother Absalom's full sister.

Absalom and Tamar were children of Maacah, daughter of Talmai, king of Geshur, an Aramaean principality northeast of the sea of Galilee, south of Maacah and north of Tob.

We saw that Amnon was so frustrated that he fell ill for Tamar. Since she was a virgin and hence protected in the harem, it seemed impossible for Amnon to have any contact with her.

We saw how Jonadab, a shrewd person, who was the son of David's brother Shimeah, suggested a scheme for Amnon either to seduce or to rape Tamar.

FROM ONE DECEPTION TO ANOTHER

So Amnon lay down and pretended to be sick. When the king came to see him, Amnon said to him,

"Please let my sister Tamar come and make a couple of cakes in my presence so I can eat from her hand."

David sent word to Tamar at the palace: "Please go to your brother Amnon's house and prepare a meal for him."

2 SAMUEL 13:6-7

Is it not ironic that Amnon used his father to perfect his demonic plan! Indeed, it was King David who brought his weight as king to bear, in response to his first son's request. He sent for Tamar to come and attend to Amnon from the harem of the women. Little did he or Tamar know that Amnon had other plans.

Many times, ladies have got raped by guys who look so innocent, guys who speak calmly and softly, guys who show so much care and love and are therefore able to conceal their true intentions.

Lady Angela had a friend who supported her emotionally and financially. One day, after church service, he invited her to his house, in the guise that he was organizing his birthday celebration to a select few friends.

She went there to help a friend by cooking for his friends. At least, as a way of repaying him for his support.

She got engaged immediately in cooking the food so she did not notice when the guy locked the gate and the exit door. Before she knew what was happening, the guy started making all sorts of efforts to force himself on her.

A major struggle began. She had to use a lantern to hit him in the face before she climbed the wall using a ladder she saw outside. Many times, ladies are deceived into very tight corners.

WHEN REASONING DOES NOT WORK.

> *When she brought them to him to eat, he grabbed her and said, "Come sleep with me, my sister!"*
>
> *"Don't, my brother!" she cried. "Don't disgrace me, for such a thing should never be done in Israel. Do not commit this outrage!*

Where could I ever go with my humiliation? And you — you would be like one of the outrageous fools in Israel! Please, speak to the king, for he won't keep me from you."

Finding herself unprotected and in the grip of the half-brother, Tamar attempted to reason with him. She even quoted the nation's history to recall the king's son to a sense of right, quoting the very words of Genesis 34:7,12...

[7] And the sons of Jacob came out of the field when they heard it: and the men were grieved, and they were very wroth, because he had wrought folly in Israel in lying with Jacob's daughter; which thing ought not to be done.

[12] Ask me never so much dowry and gift, and I will give according as ye shall say unto me: but give me the damsel to wife. Genesis 34:7,12

But Amnon was past reasoning with!

Then she spoke of the shame of the act and that the sin would meet her everywhere. Such an act would also make Amnon as " one of the fools in Israel", that is, one of those who casts away all restraint regarding the fear of God and any sense of decency. No dice. Amnon was not moved.

In desperation, she asked him to speak to the king. This was just a loose straw that she was trying to clutch at, because the marriage of half brothers and sisters was firmly forbidden in the Law:

> *The nakedness of thy sister, the daughter of thy father, or daughter of thy mother, whether she be born at home, or born abroad, even their nakedness thou shalt not uncover. The nakedness of thy father's wife's daughter, begotten of thy father, she is thy sister, thou shalt not uncover her nakedness. Leviticus 18:9,11*
>
> *And if a man shall take his sister, his father's daughter, or his mother's daughter, and see her nakedness, and she see his nakedness; it is a wicked thing; and they shall be cut off in the sight of their people: he hath uncovered his sister's nakedness; he shall bear his iniquity.*
>
> **Leviticus 20:17**

Still Amnon was not impressed. Even though it was obvious that David would not have approved of such an illicit request, he did not even agree at all.

When you put yourself in a dangerous situation, please be aware that reasoning with the beast will not work. That is why God said, "Flee youthful lusts".

FLEE STILL MEANS FLEE

> *And it house came to pass about this time, that Joseph went into the to do his business; and there was none of the men of the house there within.*

And she caught him by his garment, saying, Lie with me: and he left his garment in her hand, and fled, and got him out.
GENESIS 39:11-12

You cannot reason with a man who is high on drugs or alcohol. It is like arguing and disagreeing with a man who is high on drugs and has a revolver.

Joseph, as we saw in the above text, did not wait, he fled. Even though it meant losing some of his clothes, he still fled.

No discussion will suffice. No logic will avail. No answer will win. Just run as fast as you can. "Oh, I am strong": just run! You cannot determine what a man would do under the influence of lust. Run. Flee. Don't wait. Don't dilly dally. Escape when you can.

Satan would tell you that only a coward would run: that is a lie. Only the strong would run. The cowards would stay behind.

Why should you flee? Because you cannot reason with a man that is under the influence of lust.

Paul wrote that "it is better to marry than to BURN". Which means even God knows that lust or affection is likened to a man that is "burning". You cannot be reasoning with a man that is burning.

CONSEQUENCES OF LUSTFUL ACTIVITY.

Howbeit he would not hearken unto her voice: but, being stronger than she, forced her, and lay with her.

Then Amnon hated her exceedingly; so that the hatred wherewith he hated her was greater than the love wherewith he had loved her. And Amnon said unto her, Arise, be gone.

And she said unto him, There is no cause: this evil in sending me away is greater than the other that thou didst unto me. But he would not hearken unto her.

Then he called his servant that ministered unto him, and said, Put now this woman out from me, and bolt the door after her.

And she had a garment of divers colours upon her: for with such robes were the king's daughters that were virgins appareled. Then his servant brought her out and bolted the door after her.

And Tamar put ashes on her head and rent her garment of divers colours that was on her, and laid her hand on her head, and went on crying.

2 Samuel 13:14-19

After having his way with her, Amnon now hated her. One moment, he loved her; the next moment, he hated her. Would you really call that love? He so hated her that he drove her out.

Again, Tamar tried to do some damage control but Amnon was not interested at all. He has got what he wanted but he was not happy. He had got what he lusted after, but he was not happy.

Lust can never give you happiness. Stolen bread may look sweet but afterwards it puts sand in the mouth. You can never be satisfied with lust or illicit sex. But Satan would tell you that the more you do so, the more you will enjoy it. Satan has always been a liar and the father of lies.

Throughout all of this, David showed his own weakness and leniency because of his own moral failures and because Amnon was his firstborn son. He should have raised a storm but how can he do so, when he killed another man and appropriated his wife?

Sin incapacitates the sinner and renders him impotent. He could not do anything for two long years. Absalom waited to hear or see what the king was doing about it but nothing!

THE ULTIMATE CONSEQUENCE – DEATH!

Now Absalom commanded his young men, "Watch Amnon until he is in a good mood from the wine. When I order you to strike Amnon, then kill him. Don't be afraid. Am I not the one who has commanded you? Be strong and valiant!"

So Absalom's young men did to Amnon just as Absalom had commanded. Then all the rest of the king's sons got up, and each fled on his mule.

While they were on the way, a report reached David: "Absalom struck down all the king's sons; not even one of them survived!"

In response the king stood up, tore his clothes, and lay down on the ground, and all his servants stood by with their clothes torn.

> *But Jonadab, son of David's brother Shimeah, spoke up: "My lord must not think they have killed all the young men, the king's sons, because only Amnon is dead. In fact, Absalom has planned this ever since the day Amnon disgraced his sister Tamar.*
>
> *So now, my lord the king, don't take seriously the report that says all the king's sons are dead. Only Amnon is dead."*
>
> **2 SAMUEL 13 (CHRISTIAN STANDARD BIBLE)**

After two years, Absalom acted in revenge! He killed Amnon. Just one sexual encounter with Tamar and Amnon became dead. Amnon must have thought it's done deal only to meet his waterloo two years after. It doesn't matter how smart you think you are, if you don't deal with this matter of lust decisively you will surely bite your finger one day. If you continue to give in to lustful desires, be aware that death is imminent.

> *[15] Then when lust hath conceived, it bringeth forth sin: and sin, when it is finished, bringeth forth death.*
>
> **JAMES 1:15**

LIKE AMNON, LIKE REUBEN

There were many firstborns in the Old Testament who did not fulfil destiny but one of such men is Reuben. He was the firstborn of Jacob and that was a big deal but Reuben did something very outrageous: he slept with his father's concubine.

[21] And Israel journeyed, and spread his tent beyond the tower of Edar. [22] And it came to pass, when Israel dwelt in that land, that Reuben went and lay with Bilhah his father's concubine: and Israel heard it. Now the sons of Jacob were twelve:

Genesis 35:21-22

The Bible said, Israel heard it. What did he do? Nothing. He heard it but kept quiet. Why Reuben would do such a thing beats my imagination. After more than twenty years, Jacob spoke out and by then it was too late for Reuben.

And Jacob called unto his sons, and said, Gather yourselves together, that I may tell you that which shall befall you in the last days.

Gather yourselves together, and hear, ye sons of Jacob; and hearken unto Israel your father.

Reuben, thou art my firstborn, my might, and the beginning of my strength, the excellency of dignity, and the excellency of power:

Unstable as water, thou shalt not excel; because thou wentest up to thy father's bed; then defiledst thou it: he went up to my couch.

Genesis 49:1-4

After praising Reuben, he declared the bombshell, "Thou shalt not excel". No matter what you do afterwards, you shall not excel.

Just because of a few minutes of sexual pleasure, you shall not excel. No matter what Reuben did later (or did not do), he cannot excel. His destiny was ruined because of an hour of pleasure.

Jacob did not speak about it for so many years but when he spoke, it was really a bad day for Reuben.

The wages of sexual indiscretion may not speak that very day it was committed; but as sure as daylight, it would be spoken.

For Amnon, it was as if he had won for two years! But after two years, Absalom spoke! And revenge won!

ALL LUSTFUL ACTIVITIES ATTRACT DIVINE JUDGMENT

For every lustful activity, there is divine judgment. So many examples abound in Scriptures but we will mention some:

✓ ***One: "Sons of God coupled with daughters of men".***

> *And it came to pass, when men began to multiply on the face of the earth, and daughters were born unto them,*
>
> *That the sons of God saw the daughters of men that they were fair; and they took them wives of all which they chose.*
>
> *And the LORD said, My spirit shall not always strive with man, for that he also is flesh: yet his days shall be an hundred and twenty years.*

There were giants in the earth in those days; and also, after that, when the sons of God came in unto the daughters of men, and they bare children to them, the same became mighty men which were of old, men of renown.

And GOD saw that the wickedness of man was great in the earth, and that every imagination of the thoughts of his heart was only evil continually.

And it repented the LORD that he had made man on the earth, and it grieved him at his heart.

Genesis 6:1-6

It is believed in many circles that the sons of God mentioned above are fallen angels. If that is true, then we can further understand what Jude meant:

And the angels which kept not their first estate, but left their own habitation, he hath reserved in everlasting chains under darkness unto the judgment of the great day.

Even as Sodom and Gomorrha, and the cities about them in like manner, giving themselves over to fornication, and going after strange flesh, are set forth for an example, suffering the vengeance of eternal fire.

Likewise also these filthy dreamers defile the flesh, despise dominion, and speak evil of dignities.

Jude 1:6-8

✓ **Two: God overthrew Sodom & Gomorrah due to sexual issues.**

The sun was risen upon the earth when Lot entered into Zoar.

Then the LORD rained upon Sodom and upon Gomorrah brimstone and fire from the LORD out of heaven;

And he overthrew those cities, and all the plain, and all the inhabitants of the cities, and that which grew upon the ground.

But his wife looked back from behind him, and she became a pillar of salt.

[28] And he looked toward Sodom and Gomorrah, and toward all the land of the plain, and beheld, and, lo, the smoke of the country went up as the smoke of a furnace.

GENESIS 19:23-26,28

✓ **Three: Reuben lost his inheritance due to sexual indiscretion.**

What exactly did Reuben lose? The firstborn, the father's eldest son normally would have enjoyed the excellency of dignity, and the excellency of power by right of primogeniture. But because of the atrocity that he committed; he lost the privileges of his birthright which are:

- a double portion of the inheritance.
- the priesthood, and
- the kingdom.

The first was conferred on Joseph, the second on Levi and the third on Judah.

Why? "Unstable as water...".

That is, boiling or gushing up with lust and passion.

'Thou shalt not excel..."

He was destined for mediocrity- no judge, prophet or ruler would arise from the Reubenites.

We must stop here to ask: is it worth it? Is lust worth the trouble it creates?

Beloved, flee still means flee!

NOW THAT YOU KNOW

You have read the book. If you did so calmly in a serene and meditative environment, God would have spoken to you. We are in a battle that we cannot afford to lose.

Nothing will ruin your testimony more than sexual indiscretions.

But thank God we can still have victory over lust. How? By meditating on and applying the principles in this book. It's in your hand: why not make this book your companion?

ONE MORE **THING**

About The Author

Adebayo O. Timothy is a prolific writer, teacher of God's word and an energetic evangelist with great grace and diversities of spiritual gifts bestowed by the ministry of the Holy Spirit. He is a product of the Gospel Faith Mission Int'l (GOFAMINT) and presently serves as a District Evangelist in Lagos.. He is the visionary of the Rescue Team Mission Network International; a team of fire brand young men and women levied with the sole aim of reaching the present generation at various levels with the gospel message as well as equipping and conscripting them into Christ's army for the end time revival and global harvest. He is a conference speaker and has served in various leadership capacities ranging from tertiary institution fellowship Center, Nigeria Christian Corpers Fellowship, pastoring a church parish and other relevant bodies. He was the youth pastor for the Abuja District arm of GOFAMINT before his recent relocation to Lagos Nigeria. He is well known for his simplicity in communication. He runs an online mentorship programme where he trains audience on leadership, relationship, spiritual growth and enterprise development. He is happily married to Temitope Oluwapelumi and the union is blessed with godly children.

www.ingramcontent.com/pod-product-compliance
Lightning Source LLC
LaVergne TN
LVHW050321160826
845677LV00014B/3505

* 9 7 9 8 3 6 6 8 1 8 6 1 2 *